We Celebrate Reconciliation

The Lord Forgives

We Celebrate Reconciliation

The Lord Forgives

Christiane Brusselmans

Brian A. Haggerty

SILVER BURDETT & GINN

MORRIS

ACKNOWLEDGMENTS

All adaptations of Scripture are based on *The New American Bible with Revised New Testament.*

Excerpts from the English translation of *Rite of Penance* © 1974, International Committee on English in the Liturgy, Inc. All rights reserved.

Credits

2: l.,t.r., Silver Burdett & Ginn; b.r. Avis Mandel for Silver Burdett & Ginn. 3: t.,b. Silver Burdett & Ginn. 6: Michal Heron. 8: UPI/Bettmann Newsphotos. 9: NASA. 10:1. Camilla Smith/RAINBOW; r. Silver Burdett & Ginn. 11: Silver Burdett & Ginn. 14: t. Michal Heron; b. D&L Phillips for Silver Burdett & Ginn. 15: t. Ellis Herwig/Stock Boston; b. Silver Burdett & Ginn. 22: l. Silver Burdett & Ginn; r. Jeff Persons/Stock Boston. 23: Pam Hasegawa/Taurus Photos. 24: Silver Burdett & Ginn. 26: l. Silver Burdett & Ginn; t.r. Ken Kerbs for Silver Burdett & Ginn; b.r. Lawrence Migdale for Silver Burdett & Ginn. 30: Lawrence Migdale for Silver Burdett & Ginn. 31: Pam Hasegawa/Taurus Photos. 32: AP/Wide World Photos. 34-35: Silver Burdett & Ginn. 38: Lenore Weber/Taurus Photos. 39: Silver Burdett & Ginn. 40: Owen Franken/Stock Boston. 41: Silver Burdett & Ginn. 42: l. Silver Burdett & Ginn; t.r. Treehaus Communications, Inc./Pottebaum; b.r. Camilla Smith/RAINBOW. 43: John Lei/Stock Boston. 46: Silver Burdett & Ginn. 48-49: Silver Burdett & Ginn. 50: Treehaus Communications, Inc./Pottebaum. 51: Silver Burdett & Ginn. 52-57: Treehaus Communications, Inc./Pottebaum. 58: l. Dan McCoy/RAINBOW; t. r. Silver Burdett & Ginn; b.r. Joe Viesti for Silver Burdett & Ginn. 59: Pat Field/Bruce Coleman, Inc. 60: Karl Kummels/Shostal Associates. 61: IMAGERY. 62: Courtesy of Lamington Presbyterian Church, black walnut cross by Ken Vliet/Silver Burdett & Ginn. 67: Karen R. Preuss/Taurus Photos. 68-71: Treehaus Communications, Inc./Pottebaum. 72: Silver Burdett & Ginn. 73: Michal Heron. 75: IMAGERY.
The illustrations on pages 4-5 are by Bruce Lemerise. The illustrations on pages 12-13 are by Jane Chambliss. The illustrations on pages 18-19 are by Michele M. Epstein. The illustrations on pages 16, 20-21, 28-29, 36-37, 44-45 are by Tom Noonan.

ISBN 0-382-00639-9

Nihil Obstat
Reverend Anselm Murray, O.S.B.
Censor Librorum

Imprimatur
✠ The Most Reverend Frank J. Rodimer
Bishop of Paterson
January 3, 1989

The *nihil obstat* and *imprimatur* are official declarations that a book or pamphlet is free of doctrinal and moral error. No implication is contained therein that those who granted the *nihil obstat* and *imprimatur* agree with the contents, opinions, or statements expressed.

The contents and approach of the WE CELEBRATE RECONCILIATION program are in accord with *Basic Teachings for Catholic Religious Education* issued by the National Conference of Catholic Bishops, the *General Catechetical Directory* issued by the Sacred Congregation for the Clergy and *Sharing the Light of Faith, National Catechetical Directory for Catholics of the United States* issued by the United States Catholic Conference.

CONTENTS

1 God Calls Us to Use Our Gifts

God gives us many gifts.

Think about some of your gifts.
List them below.

Some things I enjoy doing

basketball, football, soccer, baseball, drawing,

Some things I can do well

soccer, basketball, football, baseball, drawing

Some people who are very important to me

My best friend Luke Mom, Dad, Grandpa, Grandma, sister

3

Jesus is our vine. We are the branches.

The Story of the Vine

Jesus said,
"I am the vine and you are the branches. If you
live in me and I in you, you will bear much fruit.
Just as a branch cannot bear fruit unless it remains
on the vine, so you cannot bear fruit unless you
remain in me.

If you live in me and my words stay a part of you,
you may ask what you will and it will be done
for you.

You give my Father glory in the fruit that
you bear and in becoming my **disciples**.

As the Father has loved me, so I have loved you.
Live on in my love.

Based on John 15:5–9

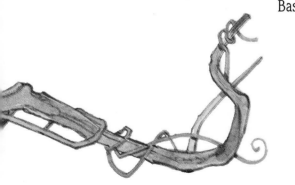

5

Jesus calls us to use our gifts to help others.

Jesus wants us to know that his life flows through us as we grow day by day in his love. Jesus uses a comparison when he says that he is the vine and we are the branches. Jesus knows that the vine feeds the branches, giving them the life that makes them lush and green. He knows that the vine gives them the nourishment they need to grow bunches of juicy grapes.

Jesus shares his life with us. At **Baptism** we receive the life of Jesus. Jesus will give us all we need to grow in his love and spread it throughout the world. This is what it means for a disciple of Jesus to bear fruit.

Read "Matthew's Story" on page 6 carefully. Think about the gifts that Matthew used to make Brian happy. Then write your own story on page 7. Describe how you use your gifts. Paste or draw a picture of yourself above the story.

Matthew's Story

Matthew is a fourth-grade student at Elm Street Elementary School. Brian is a first-grade student at the same school.

Every Friday morning, the two boys spend time together. Matthew, who is an excellent reader, tutors Brian in a special reading program.

Brian looks forward to his tutoring time. Matt helps his young friend learn new words and listens to him read aloud. With Matt's help, Brian's reading has improved. That makes both boys feel terrific!

My Story

God, Source of all life,
you have given us many gifts.
You have given us families and
friends who love and care for us.
You have given us many talents
and abilities. It is because you
love us that you sent us Jesus.
He calls us to follow him
through the gift of Baptism.
For all this we say, "Thank you!"
Amen.

God's people share their gifts with us.

Many people throughout the ages have shared their gifts with God's people. And many people today also share their gifts with others. By their examples they show us how we can share our gifts with others, too.

On these two pages are the stories of two people who used their gifts for others. You may recognize them.

Read each story carefully. Then, on the lines below each story, name one gift each person used or uses to help make God's love come alive in the world.

César Chávez

César Chávez was born to a poor family in California. His parents were migrant workers. This means that they had to move from farm to farm, picking vegetables and fruit wherever they could find work. César's family and the other migrant workers received very little pay for their long hours and hard work.

When César grew up, he knew that he must do something to help migrant workers have a better life. Many migrants were Mexican-Americans, like César and his family. These Americans were not always treated fairly by others. César wanted to do something to stop all the hurts his people suffered.

César worked very hard for migrant workers. He helped set up stores where migrants could buy things at a just price. He found teachers and lawyers to help them. Later, he helped the migrant workers organize strikes against the landowners. These strikes helped to win higher pay and better working and living conditions for the migrants.

César is still working hard today to help the migrant workers of this country. César won't stop working for migrant workers until they are treated fairly.

_____

_____

Sharon Christa McAuliffe

Sharon Christa McAuliffe was the first private citizen chosen to fly in a United States space shuttle. She was also a high-school teacher in Concord, New Hampshire, and a wife and mother of two young children. It was Christa's love of teaching that led her to the space program.

More than 11,000 people applied for the chance to fly on the space shuttle *Challenger*. Christa McAuliffe was chosen to be the first teacher to conduct a class from space. Christa believed that her experience in space would encourage and motivate all students everywhere to be the best persons they could be.

On January 28, 1986, Christa and six others boarded *Challenger*. Soon after their launching, something went wrong with the shuttle. All on board *Challenger* were killed.

Christa did not have the opportunity to teach students from space. But Christa taught the whole world a very important lesson in courage that won't soon be forgotten.

_____

_____

2 God Calls Us to Make Choices

NEWS

New Books in
School Library
– By Justin Esposito

Last week the
library received
a shipment of
75 new books.
Mr. Hiles, the
school librarian,
said that many
of the new books
are titles that
were requested
by our students

The Island of the
Blue Dolphins,
and other popular
fictional reading.
Classes can see
the new books in
a special display
next Monday. All
students are
encouraged to

SPORTS

Pam Wilson Wins Local
Gymnastics Competition
– By Jose Cardenas

Pam Wilson, a
fourth-grade student,
recently received first-
place honors in the
Hillside Gymnastics
Competition. Pam
competed with other
gymnasts in six
categories: floor
exercise, balance beam,

SPECIAL
EVENTS

Craft Show
– By Nina Fleming

Girl Scout Troup
360 is sponsoring
a craft show on
November 12
in the school
cafeteria. All craft
items are to be
submitted to Mrs.
Lazara no later
than November
5. Each entry

Band Concert
– By Lisa Keys

The high-school
band will be
performing in the
public auditorium
next Saturday and
Sunday. Both
concerts will be
at 2:00 P.M.
Tickets are avail-
at all of the
elementary schoo

We make choices every day.

When you were a little child, your parents had to decide many things for you. They often told you what to do because you were not old enough to make some decisions on your own.
1. Some of these decisions were

_____

_____

_____.

Now that you are older, you can decide many things for yourself.
2. Some of these decisions are

_____

_____

_____.

Your brothers and sisters, your grandparents, your teachers, and many other people help you every day to make choices.
3. Some of these people are

_____

_____

_____.

11

God calls us to choose what is good.

Made in God's Image

God says to us,
"I have made you a little like myself.
I have given you a mind for thinking
and a heart for loving.

I have also given you a free will
for making choices.
I have given you these gifts because I love you.

I want you to choose freely.
I want you to be able to decide what to do
and what not to do.

If you choose what is good,
you will receive my joy and peace."

Based on Sirach 17:1–11

13

We can make responsible decisions.

Our thinking minds and loving hearts enable us to make responsible choices. Our power to judge whether something is good or bad is called our **conscience**. When we choose to respond to the needs of others, Jesus promises us his joy and his peace.

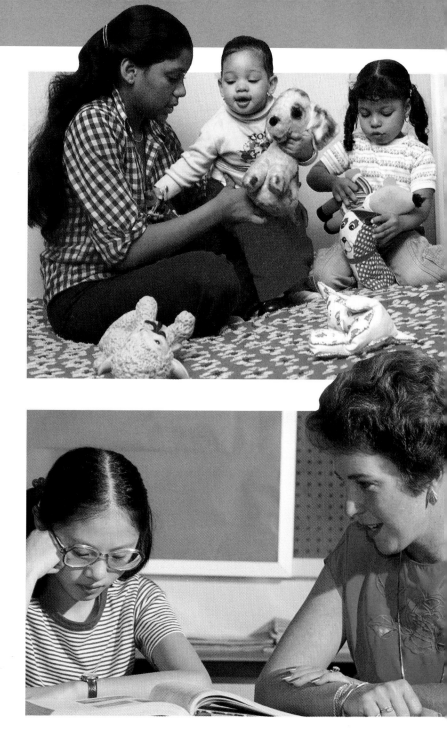

1. Some decisions I can make at home to help my parents are

Do some chores without having them tell me.

2. Some decisions I can make at school to help my teachers and classmates are

To be kind, don't be a pain, help out with your teacher

14

3. Some decisions I can make on the playground to make our games more pleasant are

Don't hert people, and have

a good time

4. Some decisions I can make in my neighborhood to help make it a better place to live are

Don't litter, clean up the

area.

God,
you call me to choose freely what is right and good. Give me the strength of your Spirit to help me make right choices. For this I say, "Thank you, Lord."
Amen.

15

Many saints have shown us how to answer God's call.

The Story of Francis

A long time ago, in the little town of Assisi, Italy, there lived a boy whose name was Giovanni Francesco Bernardone. His father was a very rich cloth merchant. He saw to it that Francis, as he was called, had everything he needed: a good home, money, and a good school. Francis also had many talents. He made friends easily. He could sing very well. He could write beautiful poems.

One day, Francis met a stranger. The man was a leper. Francis had always been afraid of people who had that disease. He asked God to help him understand what he should do. After Francis prayed, he no longer felt afraid. He knew that God was calling him to help that man and all people in need of help.

Francis was soon joined by many followers. Together they rebuilt the Church of San Damiano. A few years later, Clare and some other women also took up the same life of joy and poverty that Francis and his friends were following.

Today we know Francis of Assisi as Saint Francis. He is a saint because he freely chose to answer God's call and let the Spirit of God do great things through him.

This is a prayer that the Christian community often prays. Add to the prayer some of the needs you see around you and some ways you can respond in love.

The Prayer of Saint Francis of Assisi

Lord, make me an instrument
of your peace.
Where there is hatred,
let me sow love.
Where there is injury,
let me give pardon.
Where there is despair,
let me spread hope.
Where there is darkness,
let me shine light.
Where there is sadness,
let me bring joy.

Where there is _____
_____
let me _____
_____.

Where there is _____
_____
let me _____
_____.

Where there is _____
_____
let me _____
_____.

3 Jesus Calls Us to Follow Him

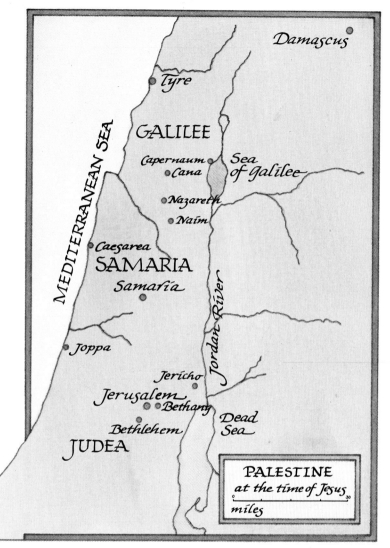

Jesus was born in Judea, in a little town called Bethlehem. He grew up in Galilee, in a town called Nazareth.

Mary and Joseph loved Jesus and cared for him every day. They taught him how to pray. They shared with him their Jewish faith. Jesus often heard these words prayed at home and in the synagogue.

The Lord your God is your only God.
You shall love God with all your heart,
and with all your spirit,
and with all your strength.
You shall love your brothers and sisters
as you love yourself.
Based on Deuteronomy 6:4–5; Leviticus 19:18

When Jesus was thirty years old, he went from town to town, bringing the good news of God's love to everyone. He told people, "Love one another, as I have loved you" (based on John 13:34).

Look at the map. Find the place where Jesus was born. Find the town where Jesus grew up.

21

Jesus invites a rich young man to follow him.

The Story of the Rich Young Man

One day a rich young man asked Jesus, "Good master, what must I do to receive everlasting life?"

Jesus answered, "You know the commandments:
Love the Lord your God.
Respect your father and mother.
Do not lie.
Do not steal.
Do not cheat or harm anyone.
Do not kill."

"Master," the young man said, "I have kept all those commandments."

Jesus looked at him with love. Then he said to him, "You only need to do one more thing. Go and sell all you have and give the money to the poor. Then come follow me."

When the rich young man heard Jesus' call, his heart was filled with sadness, and he turned away.

Jesus looked at him and said, "How hard it is for those who are rich to make their way into the kingdom of God."

Based on Matthew 19:1–23

We answer Jesus' call when we live the Beatitudes.

Like the rich young man, sometimes we don't feel like sharing. Sometimes Jesus' message seems too difficult to follow. But even when we're selfish and refuse to answer Jesus' call, God still loves us.

Jesus gives his followers ways to be happy. These ways are called the **Beatitudes**. Here are some of the Beatitudes.

Happy are we when we trust God and believe in God's love.

Happy are we when we are gentle and kind to everyone.

Happy are we when we treat others fairly and justly.

Happy are we when we are merciful and forgive others.

Happy are we when we make peace.

Happy are we when we are persecuted because we choose to do what is right.

Based on Matthew 5:3–11

1. Write about a time when you trusted God and believed in God's love.

_____

_____

_____

_____

_____

2. Write about a time when you treated others fairly and justly.

_____

_____

_____

_____

Paste or draw a picture that shows people living the Beatitudes.

God,
I want to love you with all my heart. Help me to understand your law. Your law is a light that fills my heart with love and joy. I want to do the things that please you. You are my Savior. I want to be your friend forever.
Amen.

23

Our Christian community shows us how to live the Beatitudes.

There are many ways we can live the Beatitudes by ourselves. Every day we are called to be kind and loving, caring and generous.

With others in the **Christian community,** we can do even greater things. We can join our gifts and talents to help make our community and our world better places in which to live.

Under each beatitude below, write one way your Christian community tries to live that beatitude.

Happy are we when we trust God and believe in God's love.

_____

_____

Happy are we when we console and comfort others.

_____

_____

Happy are we when we make peace.

_____

_____

Draw a picture of your Christian community working together
to answer the call of Jesus. Draw yourself into the picture.

4 Jesus Calls Us to Change Our Hearts

Sometimes our hearts are selfish and hurtful.

God makes us special. God fills us with goodness and love. The gift of God's life and presence within us is called **grace**. When we try to love others, God's goodness can be seen in us. But sometimes we may be selfish and hurtful. We may not love others. Sometimes we need a **change of heart**.

Jesus' word calls us to be less selfish, less hurtful, less careless. His words ask us to love others. If we listen to Jesus' words and try to change and become more loving, we will have a change of heart.

Read each of the following sentences. Think about a time when you wanted to do these things. Write on the lines what you chose to do instead.

I thought about not doing my chores. But I had a change of heart and instead I _did my_ _chores_ .

I wanted to change the TV show my sister was watching so I could see my favorite TV show. But I had a change of heart and instead I _watch_ _my sisster's t.v. show._

I decided to cheat on my spelling test. But I had a change of heart and instead I _didn't_ _cheat._

I thought about _hert my sister_ , but I had a change of heart and instead I _didn't_ _hert my sister_

27

Jesus invites Zacchaeus to experience a change of heart.

The Story of Zacchaeus

One day Jesus entered Jericho and was passing through the town of Jericho. Zacchaeus was the chief tax collector in Jericho and he was very rich. He had stolen most of his money from the people. Zacchaeus wanted to see who Jesus was, but he could not, because there was a big crowd of people and Zacchaeus was short.

So he ran ahead and climbed a sycamore tree, for Jesus was to pass that way. When Jesus came to that place, he looked up and said to Zacchaeus, "Zacchaeus, make haste and come down, for I must stay at your house today."

So Zacchaeus made haste and came down and welcomed Jesus joyfully to his house. When the other people and followers of Jesus saw that, they murmured, "Jesus has gone to the house of Zacchaeus to be the guest of a man who is a great sinner."

But Zacchaeus said to Jesus, "Lord, I know that I am a sinner and that I have stolen money from people. I want to change my heart. I will give half of my goods to the poor. And to anyone I have cheated, I will pay four times the money that I have stolen from them."

Jesus said to Zacchaeus, "Today peace has come to your house. Today your heart has been changed. For I have come to seek and save those who are lost."

Based on Luke 19:1–10

Like Zacchaeus, we, too, can experience a change of heart.

Zacchaeus' heart changed after meeting Jesus. We can meet Jesus when we listen closely to his words. His words can change our hearts into more loving hearts.

Do the activities on these two pages carefully. Let the story of Zacchaeus become your story, too.

Jesus called Zacchaeus to change his heart. Find Jesus' words in the story and write them on the lines below.

_____

_____

_____

Jesus calls you to change your heart. He speaks these words to you.

_____

_____

_____

Zacchaeus confesses his sins to Jesus. Find his words in the story and write them here.

_____

_____

_____

Sometimes we need to tell Jesus that we have sinned. We may have been selfish and may not have loved others. Speak to Jesus quietly in your heart.

Zacchaeus's heart was changed. What did he promise Jesus he would do? Find the words in the story and write them on the lines.

_____

_____

_____

How can your heart be changed? What can you promise Jesus you will do?

_____

_____

Jesus spoke healing words to Zacchaeus. He wants to speak those same words to you. Find them in the story. Write them here.

_____

_____

_____

Jesus,
you pardoned Zacchaeus and many other people. Pardon me, too, when I do not love my parents and family enough. Help me keep your words in my heart. Help me change my heart when I refuse to forgive others. Help me change my ways when I take what belongs to others. For this help I say "Thank you, Jesus!"
Amen.

31

In our Christian community we hear the words of Jesus and try our best to live by them.

When we forget Jesus' words and live selfishly, Jesus wants to change our hearts and make them new. We hear Jesus' word proclaimed within our Christian community. We believe that one day Jesus will say to those who follow him:

Come and enter my kingdom.

For when I was hungry,
you gave me food.

When I was thirsty.
you gave me drink.

When I was a stranger,
you took me in.

When I was naked,
you clothed me.

When I was sick,
you took care of me.

When I was in prison,
you came to see me.

Whatsoever you do
to the least of my brothers and sisters,
you do to me.

Based on Matthew 25:34–36;40

Read the sentences below. Then, on the lines provided, write one way your Christian community responds to the words of Jesus.

The Words of Jesus	We *Could* Respond by	We *Do* Respond by
When I was hungry, you gave me food.	providing a soup kitchen.	_____ _____.
When I was thirsty, you gave me drink.	working for clean water laws.	_____ _____.
When I was a stranger, you took me in.	opening our homes to exchange students.	_____ _____.
When I was naked, you clothed me.	contributing to the Thanksgiving clothing drive.	_____ _____.
When I was sick, you took care of me.	visiting sick people.	_____ _____.
When I was in prison, you came to see me.	praying for prisoners.	_____ _____.

33

5 Jesus Calls Us to Forgive One Another

① ② ③ ④

We can forgive those who hurt us.

Almost everyone knows what it is like
to be laughed at,
to be called names,
to be accused of lying,
to __be hit__ ,
to __be yelled at__ .

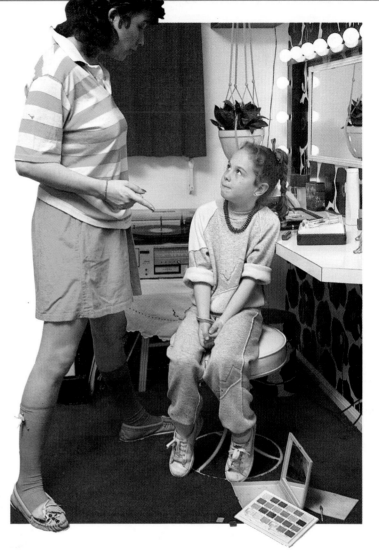

When someone hurts us, we often want to get back at that person. We may be tempted to do something mean in return. Or we may decide not to speak to the person.

Yet at the same time we are thinking about getting even, we are not happy. Deep in our hearts, we know that we should forgive the person who has hurt us.

Can you remember a time when you found it very difficult to forgive someone who hurt you? Write about it here.

_____

_____

_____

_____

_____

How did you forgive that person who hurt you?

_____

_____

_____

 *Jesus teaches us that his forgiveness is for everyone.*

Jesus Forgives a Sinner

One day, Jesus was invited to Simon's house for a meal. As he took his place at the table, a woman of the city, who was a sinner, came into Simon's house. She brought a vase filled with very expensive ointment. As she knelt at Jesus' feet, she began to wash his feet with her tears and dry them with her hair. Then she kissed his feet and anointed them with the ointment.

Now Simon, who had invited Jesus, said, "If this man was a prophet, he would know what sort of person she is, for she is a sinner."

Jesus turned toward the woman while he said to Simon, "Do you see this woman? I entered your house and you poured no water over my feet, but she has washed my feet with her tears and dried them with her hair. You did not anoint my head with oil, but she has anointed my feet. Therefore, I tell you, that her many sins are forgiven, for she has loved others greatly."

Then Jesus said to the woman,
"Your sins are forgiven.
Your faith has saved you.
Go in peace."

Based on Luke 7:36–39;44–50

37

Jesus calls us to forgive each other again and again.

What did the woman in the story do to show she was sorry?

She cleaned from feet

Think about someone who hurt you and later made up for the hurt. What did that person do to show you that he or she was truly sorry?

he said sorry and no next
time I could play

Forgiveness means pardoning sins.

In the story about the woman, Jesus shows us what it means to forgive someone. When Jesus pardoned the woman's sins, he offered her his love and friendship. He made her feel at peace.

Jesus wants us to forgive others and to make peace with them. We call this **reconciliation**.

Check all the ways you have used to show people you forgive them. Add to the list any other ways you may have used.

I have

____✓____ accepted an apology.

____✓____ treated a person in a friendly way.

____✓____ said, "I forgive you. Let's be friends."

_____ talked about what happened.

____✓____ showed them I like them.

____✓____ hugged them.

_____

_____

_____

Peter, a friend of Jesus, wanted to know how often he should forgive those who hurt him. Here is a story about Jesus' answer.

One day, Peter came to Jesus and asked, "Lord, how often should I forgive a person who sins against me? Should I forgive that person up to seven times?"

Jesus answered, "Do not say seven times, but seventy times seven times."

Based on Matthew 18:21–22

What did this mean to Jesus?

_____

_____

_____

What did this mean for Peter?

_____

_____

_____

What does this mean for me?

_____

_____

_____

Jesus,
I know that you are always ready to forgive me because you love me. Help me always to forgive others as you forgive me. For this I say, "Thank you, Jesus."
Amen.

39

Our Christian community shows us how to forgive those who hurt us.

A Story of Forgiveness

Jesus tells us that to be his followers we must forgive those who hurt us. Our Christian community gives us many people who show us what it means to forgive as Jesus forgives. Pope John Paul II is one of those people.

As the leader of the Catholic Church today, Pope John Paul has shown us how all followers of Jesus must forgive others.

Several years ago, Pope John Paul was badly hurt by gunshots fired at him. This terrible thing happened while the pope was riding past a large crowd near the Vatican. The Vatican is where the pope lives and works. The people had gathered there hoping to see the pope pass by.

One man in the crowd had a different idea. He wanted to kill Pope John Paul.

Pope John Paul was hurt very badly but he did not die. The man who shot him was put in jail.

Many months later, when the pope had recovered from his injury, he did something very special. Pope John Paul visited the man who tried to kill him. The pope told the man that he

forgave him for what he did. The man told Pope John Paul that he was sorry for hurting him.

Sometimes we need to forgive others who hurt us in a big way. Sometimes we need to forgive others for hurting us in smaller ways. Whenever we are hurt, Jesus tells us that we must forgive, over and over again.

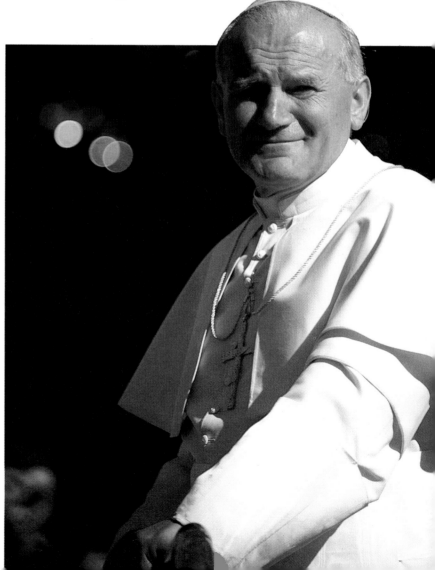

Think about those members of the Christian community who have helped you understand Jesus' message of forgiveness. Choose someone who has shown you how to forgive and write about that person here.

_____

_____

_____

_____

_____

_____

_____

Person's name_____

This person says *forgiveness* means

_____

_____

Person's name_____

This person says *forgiveness* means

_____

_____

Ask your parents, your teachers, and other adults in your Christian community what forgiveness means to them. Record their answers here.

Person's name_____

This person says *forgiveness* means

_____

_____.

41

6 Jesus Calls Us to Ask Forgiveness

It is not always easy to ask forgiveness.

Sometimes we are selfish and don't live as Jesus asks us to live. Sometimes we don't do those things we should do. Sometimes we **sin**. When we hurt ourselves or others by our selfishness, we need to ask forgiveness. It is not always easy to ask our parents to forgive us when we have done something wrong. It is hard sometimes to ask our friends to forgive us when we have hurt their feelings. It is not always easy to ask our teachers to forgive us when we have been disobedient.

Asking forgiveness of someone we have hurt can be difficult to do. But asking forgiveness is something very important that Jesus calls us to do. Asking forgiveness gives us peace.

Whom can you ask forgiveness and always be sure that those persons will forgive you?

_____

_____

_____

_____

_____

Do you ever need to ask God to forgive you?

_____

_____

_____

Are you sure that God will always forgive you?

_____

_____

_____

43

God is like a forgiving parent.

The Story of the Forgiving Father

Jesus told the following story of forgiveness.

There was a man who had two sons. The younger son said to his father, "Father, please give me the share of the family property that belongs to me." So, the father divided the property between his two sons. A few days later, the younger son gathered all he had been given and took off for a far country.

When he had spent foolishly all he had, a great famine started in that country. The boy became very hungry.

A farmer finally hired him to take care of his pigs.

The young man was so hungry he even thought of eating the pigs' food.

One day the young man said to himself, "My father's servants have plenty to eat and I am starving to death. I know what I have to do. I will get up and return to my father and say to him, 'Father, I have sinned against you. Treat me like one of your servants.' " And he got up and returned to his father.

While he was still a long way off, his father saw him coming. He ran and embraced his son and kissed him. He said to his servants, "Let us have a big celebration, for my son was dead and now he is alive; he was lost and now he is found."

Based on Luke 15:11–24;32

45

Sometimes we need to ask forgiveness.

In the Scripture story on page 45, we learn that God is like the forgiving father. We can always ask God to forgive us, too. We can speak to God in our own words and tell God how sorry we are. We can say,

Lord God,
have mercy on me because I have done wrong.

Lord God,
because you love me, forgive me all my sins.

Lord God,
pardon me and my heart shall be filled with joy.

Based on Psalm 51

Write your own prayer of sorrow, asking God to forgive you.

Lord God, please forgive me, I have don wrong and want you to forgive me. amen

Sometimes, like the younger son, we are very ungrateful for all that our parents do for us. Sometimes we do not listen to our teachers. Sometimes we quarrel with our friends.

When we have sinned, what can we do to make things right again? How can we bring back peace and friendship? How can we obey the words of Jesus that will give us happiness?

When I have disobeyed my parents, I can ask them to forgive me. This is what I might say to them.

I'm sorry I love you I did wrong

Then my mother and father might say this to me.

That's all right

Once they have forgiven me, this is how I feel.

_very good, happy, ___, ____

When I want to make up after an argument with my friends, I might say to them,

sorry lets go play

My friends might answer,

well ok, lets go

When we have made up, I feel

very good and happy.

Be happy in the Lord. Those who remain close to the Lord stand in the light. Their faces shine with joy!
Amen.

The Church invites us to ask forgiveness of God and others.

When we sin, our selfishness hurts many people. These hurt feelings, and the unhappiness they bring, may spread to many people in our family and in our Christian community. We no longer feel God's peace within us. We need to make things right again. We need to be reconciled with God and our Christian community.

Our Church community has a special way of helping us ask forgiveness and celebrating God's healing and peace. It is called the **sacrament of Reconciliation**. In this sacrament, the priest forgives us in the name of Jesus and in the name of the Christian community.

Sometimes we may want to celebrate the sacrament of Reconciliation alone with the priest. We call this an *individual* celebration of Reconciliation.

Sometimes we may want to celebrate the sacrament of Reconciliation with the rest of the Christian community. We call this a *communal* celebration of Reconciliation. See pages 68–71.

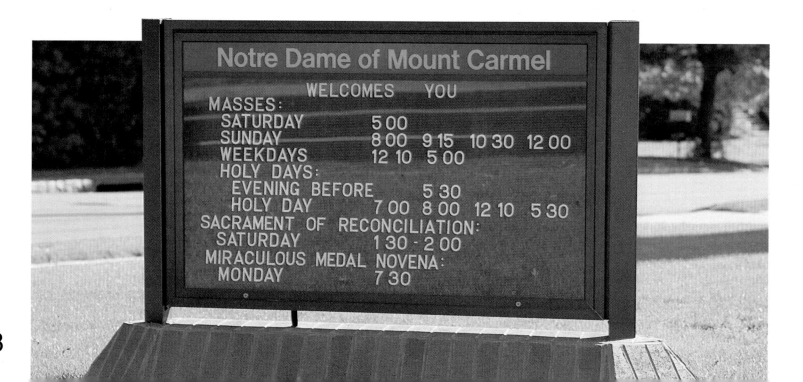

Notre Dame of Mount Carmel
WELCOMES YOU
MASSES:
SATURDAY   5 00
SUNDAY   8 00 9 15 10 30 12 00
WEEKDAYS   12 10 5 00
HOLY DAYS:
  EVENING BEFORE   5 30
  HOLY DAY   7 00 8 00 12 10 5 30
SACRAMENT OF RECONCILIATION:
  SATURDAY   1 30 - 2 00
MIRACULOUS MEDAL NOVENA:
  MONDAY   7 30

Jesus gave us a special prayer we can pray whenever we want to speak to God. This prayer mentions how we must forgive others when we ask forgiveness ourselves.

Pray this prayer with your group. Listen closely to the words that speak of forgiveness.

The Lord's Prayer

Our Father, who art in heaven,
hallowed be thy name;
thy kingdom come; thy will be done
on earth as it is in heaven.
Give us this day our daily bread;
and forgive us our trespasses
as we forgive those
who trespass against us;
and lead us not into temptation,
but deliver us from evil.
Amen.

49

7 The Church Calls Us to Celebrate the Sacrament of Reconciliation

There are times when we may want to ask God to forgive us in the **sacrament of Reconciliation.**

When we want to share in the sacrament of Reconciliation, we first remember how much God loves us. We think about what Jesus has taught and how we have lived. We ask ourselves these questions.

Do I trust in God?

Do I thank God for loving me?

Do I try to do what Jesus calls me to do?

Do I love everyone as Jesus asks me to love?

Am I always willing to forgive others and make peace?

Do I willingly share what I have with others?

This is called an **examination of conscience**.

51

Then we go to the priest individually. As we sit or kneel next to the priest, he welcomes us in the name of Jesus and in the name of the Christian community.

The priest may read from the Bible to tell us about God's mercy and forgiveness. This is called *the Reading of the Word of God.*

Then we tell the priest how we have sinned. This is called our **confession**.

The priest talks to us for a few minutes. He helps us find ways to love God more. He helps us find ways to love others as Jesus wants us to love them.

Then the priest will ask us to do a kind act or to say a prayer. This is called a **penance**. A penance helps us make up for the past. It also helps us live a better life.

The priest then invites us to tell God that we are sorry we have sinned. We may use our own words, or we may use the words of the **Act of Contrition**.

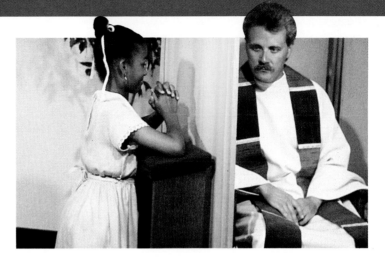

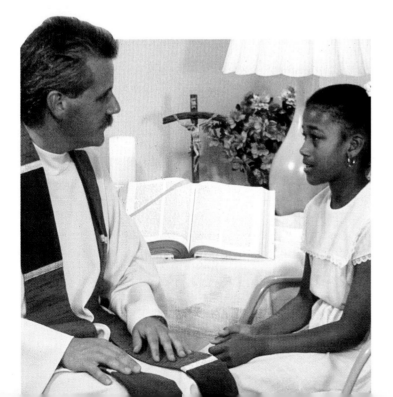

Act of Contrition

My God,
I am sorry for my sins with all my heart.
In choosing to do wrong
and failing to do good,
I have sinned against you
whom I should love above all things.
I firmly intend, with your help,
to do penance,
to sin no more,
and to avoid whatever leads me to sin.
Our Savior Jesus Christ
suffered and died for us.
In his name, my God, have mercy.

Revised *Rite of Reconciliation
of Individual Penitents*

53

After we tell God we are sorry we have sinned,
the priest lays his hand on our head and says,

"God, the Father of mercies,
through the death and resurrection of his Son
has reconciled the world to himself
and sent the Holy Spirit among us
for the forgiveness of sins;
through the ministry of the Church
may God give you pardon and peace,
and **I absolve you from your sins
in the name of the Father, and of the Son,
and of the Holy Spirit.**"
Amen.

Revised *Rite of Reconciliation
of Individual Penitents*

The priest makes the Sign of the Cross over us. This prayer of forgiveness prayed by the priest is called **absolution**.

55

Together, the priest and I praise and thank God. We tell God how happy we are because God always loves us. We tell Jesus how much we want to answer his call. We ask Jesus to help us as we try to bring his love to everyone. We remember our penance and do it now or as soon as possible.

God,
how happy I am now that you have forgiven me. I know that you show me the way. I know that you look after me. Help me to bring your love into my family, my school, and my neighborhood. For all this, I say, "Thank you, Lord." Amen.

Now that we are reconciled and forgiven, there is a new joy and peace within us. We are now one with God and one with all those whom God asks us to love and care about.

Decorate the border of this prayer to show your new-found joy after Reconciliation. Pray the prayer with your group.

Merciful God,
you chose us to be your children,
to be holy in your sight and happy in your presence.

Welcome us as a loving Father
so that we may share the joy and love
of your holy Church.

We ask this through Christ, our Lord.
Amen.

57

8 The Spirit of Jesus Helps Us Share Our Gifts

la comunidad – community
los vecinos – neighbors
los amigos – friends
la familia – fami

Jesus gives us his Spirit.

Those who belong to Jesus have the Spirit of Jesus within them.

The Spirit of Jesus opens our hearts to joy, peace, patience, kindness, generosity, trust, and gentleness.

Based on Galatians 5:22–23

59

The Spirit of Jesus helps us carry out our mission.

In the sacrament of Reconciliation, we receive God's pardon and peace. God's love and forgiveness help us use our gifts for others and let them know how much God loves them.

We are sent out again to bring God's love and forgiveness to everyone we meet. The Holy Spirit, the Spirit of Jesus, helps us carry out our mission of sharing God's love and peace.

The Spirit of Jesus helps us look at the world and see the beauty and goodness that God has placed there. The Spirit of Jesus helps us praise and thank God who gives us the world to enjoy.

The Spirit of Jesus helps us see the needs and the sufferings of so many people in the world.

The Spirit of Jesus helps each of us use our special gifts so that we can help make the world a better place for everyone.

Complete this prayer. Ask the Spirit of Jesus to help you use your gifts to make this a better world.

Spirit of Jesus,

thank you for ————————————————————————

————————————————————————————— .

Help me to ————————————————————————

————————————————————————————— .

Encourage me when ——————————————————

————————————————————————————— .

Be with me as ————————————————————

————————————————————————————— .

Teach me how ————————————————————

————————————————————————————— .

Never stop ——————————————————————

————————————————————————————— .

Amen.

Review

Theme 1: God Calls Us to Use Our Gifts

We can respond to God's love for us by using well the gifts God has given us. We use our gifts well when we use them to help others.

Theme 2: God Calls Us to Make Choices

God calls us to choose what is good so that we can respond to the needs of others. God has given us thinking minds and loving hearts to help us make good choices.

Theme 3: Jesus Calls Us to Follow Him

We can answer Jesus' call to follow him by living the Beatitudes. If we live the Beatitudes and listen to Jesus' words, we will find joy.

Theme 4:   Jesus Calls Us
to Change Our Hearts

Sometimes we need a change of heart because we become selfish and refuse to answer Jesus' call. Jesus will always forgive us when we ask. Jesus wants to change our hearts and make them new.

Theme 5:   Jesus Calls Us
to Forgive One Another

To be reconciled means to forgive those who hurt us and to be united to them in friendship. Jesus asks us to forgive others as he has forgiven us.

Theme 6:   Jesus Calls Us
to Ask Forgiveness

The sacrament of Reconciliation is a special way our Christian community asks forgiveness and celebrates God's healing and peace. In this sacrament, the priest forgives us in the name of Jesus and in the name of the Christian community.

Theme 7:   The Church Calls Us
to Celebrate the
Sacrament of Reconciliation

When I celebrate the sacrament of Reconciliation, Jesus promises us his forgiveness and healing. He gives us a new joy and peace. He reconciles us to God and to the Christian community.

Theme 8:   The Spirit of Jesus Helps Us
Share Our Gifts

The sacrament of Reconciliation sends us out again to use our gifts for others and let others know how much God loves them. The Holy Spirit helps us use our gifts to make the world a better place for everyone.

Glossary

absolution
the prayer of forgiveness prayed by the
priest in the sacrament of Reconciliation (page 55)

Baptism
one of the sacraments of initiation through which
new members are welcomed into the Christian
community (page 6)

Beatitudes
the teachings of Jesus on how to live happily;
how Jesus lived (page 22)

change of heart
the call of Jesus that asks us to become more
loving and less selfish (page 27)

Christian community
the family of Jesus we belong to through Baptism
(page 24)

confession
sharing with the priest in the sacrament of
Reconciliation how we may have sinned (page 53)

conscience
our power to judge whether something is
good or bad (page 14)

Contrition, Act of
a prayer of sorrow for our sins (page 53)

disciple

a friend and follower of Jesus (page 5)

examination of conscience

thinking about what we have said and done and how we may have sinned (page 51)

forgiveness

the pardoning of our sins (page 38)

grace

the gift of God's own life and presence (page 27)

penance

a kind act we do or a prayer we say that helps us make up for the past and do better in the future (page 53)

reconciliation

making peace through sorrow and forgiveness (page 38)

sacrament of Reconciliation

a sacrament that celebrates in a special way the love and forgiveness of God, brings us healing and peace, and reconciles us to God and to the Christian community (page 48)

sin

to choose to act selfishly; to turn away from God and choose not to love (page 27)

Day by Day

Day by day the words of Scripture help us walk on the path of joy and peace.

Love the Lord with all your heart.
(based on Deuteronomy 6:5)

Do I think about God often?

Do I pray to God every day?

Do I praise and thank God for loving me?

Do I care for all the beautiful things God has given me?

Do I ask God to forgive me when I do something wrong?

Jesus tells us, "Love one another as I have loved you."
(based on John 13:34)

Do I thank God for all the people who care for me?

Do I help my parents without being told?

Do I ask my parents and teachers to forgive me?

Do I ask my friends to forgive me?

Am I kind to everyone?

Do I try to be friends with those children who do not have any friends?

Do I try to treat everyone fairly?

Do I try to bring peace where there is fighting?

Do I sometimes take what is not mine: money, books, toys?

God says to us, "I have made you a little like myself."

(based on Sirach 17:1)

Do I use the gifts God has given me?

Do I use my talents and gifts for others?

Do I take good care of myself?

Do I use well the good mind God has given me?

Do I love myself as a special child of God?

Act of Contrition

My God,
I am sorry for my sins with all my heart.
In choosing to do wrong,
and failing to do good,
I have sinned against you
whom I should love above all things.
I firmly intend, with your help,
to do penance,
to sin no more,
and to avoid whatever leads me to sin.
Our Savior Jesus Christ
suffered and died for us.
In his name, my God, have mercy.

Revised *Rite of Reconciliation
of Individual Penitents*

Act of Contrition

Lord Jesus, Son of God,
have mercy on me, a sinner.

Revised *Rite of Reconciliation
of Individual Penitents*

Prayers of Praise

Here are some prayers we can find in the Book of Psalms.

Rejoice in the Lord and sing for joy, friends of God.
(based on Psalm 32:1–7, 10–11)

Great and wonderful are all your works, Lord.
(based on Revelation 15:3–4)

I will sing to my God all the days of my life.
(based on Psalm 146:2–10)

Fill us with your love, O Lord, and we will sing for joy!
(based on Psalm 90:14)

It is good for me to be with the Lord.
(based on Psalm 73:28)

Happy are they who follow the law of the Lord!
(based on Psalm 119:1)

The Lord is loving and kind: God's mercy is forever.
(based on Psalm 100:2–5)

My spirit rejoices in my God.
(based on Isaiah 61:10–11)

Praise the Lord and call upon God's name.
(based on Isaiah 12:1–6)

Blessed be God who chose us in Christ.
(based on Ephesians 1:3–10)

69

Living your Faith

The Beatitudes

Happy are we when we trust God
and believe in God's love.

Happy are we when we comfort others.

Happy are we when we are gentle
and kind to everyone.

Happy are we when we treat others
fairly and justly.

Happy are we when we are merciful
and forgive others.

Happy are we when we keep God's
words in our minds and hearts.

Happy are we when we make peace.

Happy are we when we are persecuted
because we choose to do what is right.

Based on Matthew 5:3–11

The Ten Commandments

1. I, the Lord, am your God.
   You shall not have other gods besides me.

2. You shall not take the name of the Lord your
   God in vain.

3. Remember to keep holy the sabbath day.

4. Honor your father and mother.

5. You shall not kill.

6. You shall not commit adultery.

7. You shall not steal.

8. You shall not bear false witness against your
   neighbor.

9. You shall not covet your neighbor's wife.

10. Your shall not covet anything that belongs to
    your neighbor.

Based on Exodus 20:2–17

The Great Commandment

You shall love the Lord, your God,
with all your heart,
with all your soul,
with all your strength,
and with all your mind.
You shall love your neighbor as yourself.
> Based on Deuteronomy 6:4–5;
> Leviticus 19:18

Corporal Works of Mercy

1. Feed the hungry.

2. Give drink to the thirsty.

3. Clothe the naked.

4. Visit those in prison.

5. Shelter the homeless.

6. Visit the sick.

7. Bury the dead.

71

When We Celebrate the Sacrament with God's Family

Gathering Rite

As we gather together, we sing and pray. Together, the Christian community remembers how much God loves us. We recall how Jesus taught us to live and love. We are now ready to celebrate God's healing and forgiveness.

Celebration of the Word of God

We listen carefully to the word of God as it is proclaimed. The Scripture stories remind us of how special we are because we belong to God and to God's family. We hear, too, how we should live as brothers and sisters of Jesus.

The presider explains the Scriptures to us. We learn what God's word means for us.

After we have listened to God's word, the presider asks us to bring to mind those good things we have said or done when we have tried to love others well. Next, the presider asks us to recall those words or actions which may have been selfish and unloving, those times when we chose not to love as Jesus taught us.

73

Rite of Reconciliation

Together, the Christian community prays for forgiveness. We remember how much God wants to forgive us and so we ask for God's pardon and peace. We pray the prayer that Jesus taught us, the Lord's Prayer.

Individual Confession and Absolution

Now we are ready to go individually to the priest and talk about those words or actions for which we feel sorry. We ask the priest to celebrate God's forgiveness with us.

The priest helps us see how we can change our hearts. Together, we decide on a penance, a prayer or a kind action which will help us make up for the past.

The priest extends his hand over us and says the prayer of absolution.

Proclamation of Praise

Together, the Christian community thanks and praises God for the forgiving love we have received. We may sing a song of praise.

Concluding Rite

As we prepare to leave the church, the priest wishes us God's blessing and peace. We sing a song of praise as we go forth to love God by loving others.

75

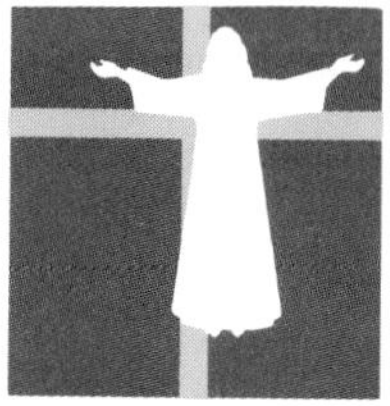

On the 2nd day of December,

in the year of Our Lord 1990

in Holy Spirit Church

located in

Indianapolis, Indiana.

Kyle Gilliatt
Child

celebrated the sacrament of Reconciliation

for the first time.

Chris Collier
Catechist

Wm. Munshower
Pastor

Diana M. Gilliatt
Neal E. Gilliatt
Parent

B C D E F G H I J—W—96 95 94 93 92 91 90 89